AF428277

YOUR TWIN FLAME LOVE STORY

A Guided Love Story Format For Manifesting Harmonious Union

JASMINE RANA

Life Coach

CONTENT

- PREFACE — 3
- THE SPLIT-UP — 9
- ONSET OF SELF-LOVE — 14
- SELF-CARE IS HAPPINESS — 21
- OVERCOMING THE SHADOW SIDE — 25
- A DATE WITH HERSELF — 29
- UNLEASHING HER CREATIVE SIDE — 33
- VIBRATING LOVE — 41
- DREAM DESTINATION WITH MY TWIN FLAME — 43
- INNER CHILD HEALING — 57
- CLEARING ENERGY BLOCKS IN ULTIMATE LOVE UNION — 96
- HEALING MY TWIN FLAME CONNECTION — 129
- MANIFESTING ULTIMATE LOVER'S TEXT MESSAGE AND UNION — 135
- ABOUT THE AUTHOR — 139

PREFACE

If you want to manifest love and attract someone into your life, you must keep yourself truly happy. Never expect others to make you happy. Engage in activities that get your endorphins flowing, spend quiet time raising your vibration, read empowering books and success stories of union, get plenty of sleep, create vision boards, and start scripting your harmonious union and relationship as if it's happening now. Visit places that inspire you—whether a spiritual or religious site, nature, or a moving film. Spend time with friends and family who believe in you and uplift your spirit.

Free yourself from limiting beliefs that have held you back since childhood. You'll be surprised at what can emerge from releasing old patterns. Let go of your fears to make space for the Universe to respond swiftly.

Steps for Self-Care and Manifestation:

Step 1: Surrender to the Universe

Decide to hand over control to the Universe. Summon the Universe and say, "I trust the

Universe to know my heart's desire and that it will take care of me." Have unwavering faith and no longer doubt or worry about your Twin Flame or specific person. Once you give full control to the Universe, you will instantly feel better.

Step 2: Practice Forgiveness

Forgive your ex for any harsh words, ignorance, lack of communication, or breakup. Each time you think of them, say, "*I love you too,*_________________ *[Twin Flame's Name]*." Send them loving energy and thoughts each time you say this.

Step 3: Visualize Your Union

Imagine your life together with your Twin Flame. Picture both of you laughing, looking at each other with love, and sharing an amazing, harmonious relationship. Each time you think about and script this in your journal, smile and feel happy.

Step 4: Detach and Trust

Feel detached from your desired outcome, relaxed, confident, and certain about your manifestation arriving. Trust that they will return and that it will feel amazing. Stop thinking about them constantly; just let it go and feel at peace.

Focus on all the things you love about them and your relationship. Count your blessings for the happy moments you shared and the things they did for you.

Self-Love and Empowerment:

To attract back someone you love, you must prioritize yourself. Choose yourself and make yourself a priority. If you want to manifest love, you need to vibrate love. Start by loving yourself! Every morning and evening, do mirror exercises: stand in front of the mirror and tell yourself how much you love yourself. This practice will help you appreciate and empower yourself. Write down all the positive things about yourself and why someone would be lucky to have you. Affirm that you and your Twin Flame are back together.

Prioritize yourself and do what's best for you. Engage in activities that make you happy, practice self-love, self-healing, and self-care. Remember, you don't need anyone else to make you happy. You are the lead actor in your life's movie, so take charge.

The Power of Letting Go:

To attract someone you love back, you must be willing to let go. It sounds scary, but if you keep missing them or wanting them, you send vibrations of lack to the Universe. The Universe will then mirror this lack back to you. Letting go is essential. Have faith that the Universe has your best interests at heart and surrender all to it. This approach makes the manifestation process quicker and with less resistance.

Scripting Your Love Story:

Start scripting in your journal as if you are already a couple again. Write down how thankful you are to have them in your life, list all the wonderful qualities you love about them, and describe how happy they make you feel. Let go of the feeling of not having them, and soon they will come back. You won't believe how quickly your union happens!

Accept that you create your world. Let go, and that's when the magic begins. It all happens when you least expect it and are totally distracted from them.

Use this time of separation for holistic self-growth and healing. Follow the exercises mentioned in each chapter to raise your vibration and align your energy with the union you desire. You are just the right vibration away from your union.

Let's rewrite your love story together with this guided story format to manifest your love back. Your union is within reach, and it all starts with loving yourself.

_______'S
TWIN FLAME
LOVE STORY

THE SPLIT-UP

Once upon a time, a girl named
______________________[Your Name] found
herself heartbroken after being separated from
her Twin Flame, [Twin Flame's Name]. The
pain was unbearable, and she couldn't get him
off her mind. Sleepless nights and a sense of
emptiness filled her days, making life feel like
a never-ending struggle.

Her unawakened Twin Flame had stopped
communicating and was denying their love.
He needed space for his own healing and a
sense of direction to become a whole and
complete partner. Often distracted and misled
by others, he wandered in the wrong
direction, unaware of the true depth of their
connection.

But ______________[Your Name] knew in
her heart that one day, her Twin Flame would
awaken to his real self, realize their profound
love, and return to her as a better, wiser
person. Meanwhile, she chose to let him go,
respecting his need for space and privacy. She
understood that her own healing and
awakening were just as important and decided
to embark on her journey of self-love.

The Path to Healing

Determined to be ready for their harmonious union, ______________________[Your Name] started focusing on herself. She knew that by healing and nurturing her own soul, she would raise her vibration and align herself with the love she desired. Here's how her story of self-love unfolded:

Step 1: Surrender to the Universe

One quiet evening, as the sun set, ______________________[Your Name] sat under a beautiful, old tree in her favorite park. She closed her eyes, took a deep breath, and whispered to the Universe, "I trust you to know my heart's desire and take care of me." With each breath, she felt a growing sense of peace, knowing that the Universe was aligning everything perfectly.

Step 2: Practice Forgiveness

Every time thoughts of her Twin Flame surfaced, she practiced forgiveness. She would sit in a serene room filled with soft candlelight and say, "I love you too, [Twin Flame's Name]." She sent him loving energy and thoughts, releasing any bitterness and allowing her heart to heal.

Step 3: Visualize a Harmonious Union

Each night, before drifting off to sleep, _______________[Your Name] would visualize her life together with her Twin Flame. She pictured them laughing, looking at each other with love, and sharing a harmonious relationship. She kept a journal by her bed where she scripted their love story, filling each page with vivid details and joyous emotions.

Step 4: Letting Go and Trusting

Learning to let go was a challenge, but [Your Name] knew it was necessary. She imagined herself by a tranquil lake, feeling the serenity wash over her. She trusted that her manifestation was on its way and stopped obsessing over her Twin Flame, finding peace in the present moment.

Embracing Self-Love

To truly attract love, _______________[Your Name] realized she needed to love herself first. She began each day with mirror exercises, looking into her eyes and saying, "I love you." She wrote down all the wonderful qualities she possessed and affirmed that she was worthy of love. This practice empowered her, reinforcing her self-worth.

She filled her days with activities that made her happy—spending time with supportive friends and family, engaging in physical activities, reading inspiring books, and visiting places that lifted her spirit. She prioritized her well-being and allowed herself to heal.

The Power of Letting Go

__________________[Your Name] understood that to attract her Twin Flame back, she had to be willing to let go. It was scary, but she knew that holding on to the feeling of lack would only attract more lack. By surrendering to the Universe, she trusted that everything would fall into place.

Scripting Her Love Story

In her journal, __________________[Your Name] scripted as if she and her Twin Flame were already a couple. She wrote about how thankful she was to have him in her life, listed his wonderful qualities, and described the happiness he brought her. She let go of the feeling of not having him, trusting that their union was imminent.

As _____________________[Your Name]
continued her journey of self-love and
healing, she felt her vibration rise and her
heart open. She knew that her Twin Flame
union was just a vibration away. Embracing
the magic of the present moment, she lived
her life with joy and confidence, knowing that
her ultimate lover would return when the time
was right.

And so, _________________[Your Name]'s
story of self-love became a beautiful journey
of healing and transformation, paving the way
for the reunion she always believed in. Her
faith in the Universe and dedication to her
own growth created a powerful love story that
was destined to unfold.

ONSET OF SELF-LOVE

___________________[Your Name] woke up one morning with a nudge to love herself more and awaken to her true self. "It feels like miracles are waiting for me, and I am feeling excited for no reason," she said, a smile spreading across her face as she embraced the promise of a new day.

Determined to nurture this newfound excitement, ___________________[Your Name] began her day with her gratitude diary. She sat by the window, letting the warm sunlight wash over her, and started counting her blessings. She listed every small and big thing she was thankful for—her supportive friends, her loving family, the beauty of nature, and the moments of joy she experienced daily. This practice filled her heart with appreciation and set a positive tone for the day ahead.

With her heart full of gratitude, ___________________[Your Name] set her goals for physical and mental fitness and inner child healing. She knew that to clear her vibration and align herself with the love she desired, she needed to focus on her overall well-being.

Step 1: Setting Physical Fitness Goals

___________________[Your Name] understood the importance of taking care of her body. She planned a routine that included activities she enjoyed, like morning jogs in the park, yoga sessions that stretched and strengthened her body, and dance classes that filled her with joy and energy. She set small, achievable goals for herself, knowing that each step forward was a step towards her higher self.

Step 2: Embracing Mental Fitness

For mental fitness, ___________________[Your Name] incorporated mindfulness and meditation into her daily routine. She found a quiet corner in her home, where she could sit comfortably, close her eyes, and focus on her breath. This practice helped her clear her mind, reduce stress, and connect with her inner peace. She also committed to reading empowering books and success stories of twin flame unions, which provided her with inspiration and hope.

Step 3: Inner Child Healing

___________________[Your Name] recognized that healing her inner child was crucial for clearing her vibration. She began with simple exercises, such as writing letters to her younger self, and expressing love and understanding. She visualized herself comforting her inner child, assuring her that she was safe, loved, and worthy. This process helped ____________________[Your Name] release old fears and limiting beliefs that had been holding her back.

Creating a Vision Board

To keep her motivation high, ____________________[Your Name] decided to create a vision board. She gathered magazines, scissors, glue, and a large poster board. She spent an afternoon cutting out images and words that resonated with her dreams and aspirations. Her vision board included pictures of happy couples, serene nature scenes, affirmations of self-love, and symbols of success and abundance. Placing the board where she could see it every day, she felt a surge of excitement and determination to manifest her desires.

Scripting Her Harmonious Union

Each evening, ____________________[Your Name] spent time scripting her harmonious union with her twin flame as if it were happening now. She wrote about their joyful moments together, their deep connection, and the love they shared. She described their harmonious relationship in vivid detail, feeling the emotions as if they were real. This practice not only brought her joy but also aligned her vibration with the union she longed for.

Seeking Inspiration

_______________[Your Name] made it a point to seek inspiration regularly. She visited spiritual and religious places, walked in nature, and watched movies that moved her heart. These activities filled her with positivity and reinforced her belief in the miracles awaiting her.

Surrounding Herself with Positive Energy

She surrounded herself with friends and family who believed in her and supported her journey. Their love and encouragement uplifted her spirit and kept her vibration high. She learned to set boundaries, ensuring that she spent her time with people who brought out the best in her.

Embracing Self-Love

Every morning and evening, _______________[Your Name] stood in front of the mirror and told herself, "I love you." She listed all the positive things about herself and affirmed that she was worthy of love and happiness. This daily practice of self-love empowered her and strengthened her self-worth.

As _________________[Your Name] continued her journey of self-care, she felt a profound transformation within herself. The pain of separation began to fade, replaced by a sense of peace and excitement for the future. She knew that by loving and healing herself, she was not only preparing for her twin flame union but also creating a life filled with joy and abundance.

_________________[Your Name]'s journey was a beautiful reminder that true love begins within. By prioritizing her well-being and embracing self-love, she was aligning herself with the vibration of her desires. Each step she took brought her closer to the harmonious union she always believed in.

_________________'s **Gratitude List:**

   1. "I am grateful for my good health."

   2.

   3.

4.

5.

6.

7.

8.

9.

10.

She eats her healthy breakfast and heads to her work. While she's at <u>work/college</u> she misses her twin flame. Whenever her Twin Flame comes to her mind, she sends him love and light vibrationally and says in her mind *"Love and Light to you my Love"*.

SELF-CARE IS HAPPINESS

Each day ________________ *(your name)* starts her day with self-care. She has started loving herself more and more with each passing day.
She starts the day with a morning gratitude journaling ritual to spending time in nature and an evening bath with essential oils.
She knows how to clear her energy and stay grounded within her own energy.

She keeps working towards her goals and career. She is manifesting new ideas to expand her career, achieve her goals and have a peaceful work environment.
She starts making a list of her desired career, and the lifestyle which is associated with the career and goals to achieve:

________________'s **Desired Career List:**

1. Peaceful and fun work environment.

2.____

After making the list she gives thanks
to the universe and surrenders the
outcome to the universe and divine
timing.

Later one day she decided to work on
her physical fitness too. She makes a
diet plan with a balanced diet in her
mind, cutting off sugary and junk food.
She takes out time for cardio and
exercises to get in good shape.
"When you look good you feel good too",
she said.

OVERCOMING THE SHADOW SIDE

After a few months of self-love and care and dedicating herself to growing her career and achieving her goals she was glowing from within. She was releasing her old negative-limiting beliefs about relationships, love, spouse, self, money, health, her abilities, etc...

She made a list of negative beliefs she learned from her parents, caretaker, and others or after experiencing traumatic incidents and replacing them with a positive affirmation:

1. Money comes after struggle and hard work.
   (Negative Belief)
   Money comes easily and effortlessly.
   (Positive affirmation)
2. I get emotionally unavailable partners.
   (Negative Belief)
   I attract a genuine and caring loving partner.
   (Positive Affirmation)

____

____

____

She releases her negative beliefs one by one as she remembers them at any time of the day. To release those suppressed beliefs first she accepts that they are there and then she says this affirmation in her mind to release it from inside herself, " I realise this belief out of my mind, body and soul and this no longer controls me."
As she does this every day, she feels lighter and lighter. She notices a positive difference in her and her life and her health get better and better.

A DATE WITH HERSELF

As she is feeling good about herself and feeling the energy of love she starts pampering herself and treats herself with things she likes. She would cheer herself up with treats like her favourite dessert, shopping, skincare, and spending time in nature or with friends.

______________'s **To-Do List for Self-Love**

1. *Eat my favourite ice cream today.*
2. *Watch a rom-com movie tonight.*

__________(your name) has realized that she's the only person who can keep and make herself happy. She has to keep her cup of love full so that she can share her love and be whole and complete rather than a needy person who just wants to take and take to fill her own cup of love. She understands now that this would repel her twin flame, so to attract him back she needs to be in her own energy, keeps her cup of love full, be whole and complete, and do inner healing work.

UNLEASHING HER CREATIVE SIDE

_________________[Your Name] woke up one morning with a profound feeling to tap into her creative side once again. She felt an irresistible urge to express herself through art and creativity, knowing that this would be a powerful way to heal and manifest her desires.

Determined to embrace her creative energy, she decided to dance often, fearlessly, and privately in her bedroom. The music moved her, and as she danced, she felt a sense of liberation and joy. Each movement helped her release pent-up emotions, filling her with happiness and peace.

Next, she started sketching and painting again. She set up a cozy corner in her room with her art supplies and let her imagination flow. She painted vibrant images that reflected her dreams and desires. Each brushstroke brought her closer to the vision of her harmonious union.

To add another layer of joy, _________________[Your Name] began singing romantic songs on karaoke and sing-along videos with lyrics. She let her voice express the love and longing in her heart, feeling the music resonate deep within her soul.

Creating a Vision Through Art

_________________[Your Name] realized that

drawing out her desires was a powerful creative process. She started sketching scenes she wanted to experience with her Twin Flame:

- **Romantic Dates**: She drew pictures of cozy cafes, beachside dinners, and candlelit tables where they would share intimate moments.

- **Vacations**: She painted beautiful landscapes of exotic destinations they would explore together, feeling the excitement of their adventures.

- **Festive Get-Togethers**: She illustrated Christmas celebrations, festive gatherings, and holiday traditions they would enjoy as a couple.

- **Union**: She depicted the moment of their union, the joy in their eyes, and the love that radiated between them.

- **Romantic Proposal**: She sketched a romantic proposal scene, capturing the emotion and happiness of that special moment.

- **Life Together**: She painted a future life with her Twin Flame, a home filled with love, laughter, and harmony.

- **Receiving Gifts**: She drew herself receiving a heartfelt written note or a special gift from her Twin Flame, feeling the warmth and affection in each gesture.

The Power of Creative Visualization

Drawing and painting her desires became a powerful manifestation tool for _________________[Your Name]. She believed in the law of attraction and knew that by visualizing and creating art, she was aligning her energy with her dreams. Each piece of art she created was a step closer to bringing her desires into reality.

Embracing Joy and Healing

Through her creative endeavors, _________________[Your Name] found immense joy and a sense of fulfillment. She felt her vibration rise as she immersed herself in art, dance, and music. This creative process not only helped her heal but also strengthened her belief in the power of self-expression.

As _____________[Your Name] continued to tap into her creative energy, she felt a profound transformation within herself. The pain of separation began to fade, replaced by a sense of excitement and anticipation for the future. She knew that by embracing her creativity and expressing her desires through art, she was aligning herself with the love she longed for.

Her journey of self-love and creative expression was a beautiful reminder that true happiness comes from within. By nurturing her creative side and visualizing her dreams, _________________[Your Name] was manifesting a life filled with joy, love, and harmony. She believed wholeheartedly that her Twin Flame union was just a creative expression away.

My Dream Date with Twin Flame Sketch:

Vacation With My Twin Flame Sketch:

Receiving Token of Love (gift) from my Beloved

Sketch:

Happy Moments with My Twin Flame:

List of Favourite Love songs for Karaoke:

1.

2.

3.

4.

5.

6.

7.

8.

9.

10.

11.

12.

13.

14.

15.

16.

17.

18.

19.

20.

21.

22.

23.

24.

25.

26.

VIBRATING LOVE

To vibrate in the constant energy of love when _____________ (*your name*) felt low due to any things negative around or lack of visible physical development for their union, whereas it's happening in the background, watching romantic movies at night evoked love vibration within her.

"Romantic movies evoke loving, forgiving, understanding and cooperating feelings within us."

The feeling of love and yearning for the beloved in the movie evokes similar feelings within her and aligns her with loving energy.

These movies also made _____________________(*your name*) more hopeful and gave her warm feeling. It made her believe in the power of love, patience and divine timing.

It made her believe good things are waiting for her to experience with her twin flame.

She kept adding romantic movies to watch on her list for every night.

_____________'s Romantic Movie To Watch:

1. Leap Year (2010)
2. The Holiday (2006)
3. Blended (2014)
4. The Lake House (2006)
5.
6.
7.
8.
9.
10.
11.
12.
13.
14.
15.
16.
17.
18.
19.
20.
21.
22.
23.
24.
25.

DREAM DESTINATION WITH MY TWIN FLAME

One day ___________________ *(your name)* was going through a travel magazine with romantic, beautiful and exotic destinations. She makes a list of dream destinations to visit with her twin flame across the world. She makes a detailed list of an itinerary for each country she wants to visit with her twin flame.

She visualizes vacation with her twin flame to her favourite destinations. Those vacations create new happy memories, make them stronger as a couple, learn about each other more, increase romance in their relationship and make both realise the importance of what they have together.
She draws and journals down her ideal vacation and its itinerary with happy moments with her twin flame. She researched the visa procedures for her nationality and hotels/resorts abroad.

_________________'s
DREAM HOLIDAY

I am going to:

Going with:

Why I chose this location:

How will I get there (conveyance):

Activities I will do with Him:

What I will pack with me:

TRAVEL ITINERARY
Things to Buy, Eat and Visit

DAY 1	
DAY 2	
DAY 3	
DAY 4	
DAY 5	

DREAM HOLIDAY

I am going to:

Why I chose this location:

How will I get there (conveyance):

Activities I will do with Him:

What I will pack with me:

TRAVEL ITINERARY
Things to Buy, Eat and Visit

DAY 1	
DAY 2	
DAY 3	
DAY 4	
DAY 5	

DREAM HOLIDAY

I am going to:

Why I chose this location:

How will I get there (conveyance):

Activities I will do with Him:

What I will pack with me:

TRAVEL ITINERARY
Things to Buy, Eat and Visit

DAY 1	
DAY 2	
DAY 3	
DAY 4	
DAY 5	

DREAM HOLIDAY

I am going to:

Why I chose this location:

How will I get there (conveyance):

Activities I will do with Him:

What I will pack with me:

TRAVEL ITINERARY

Things to Buy, Eat and Visit

DAY 1	
DAY 2	
DAY 3	
DAY 4	
DAY 5	

DREAM HOLIDAY

I am going to:

Why I chose this location:

How will I get there (conveyance):

Activities I will do with Him:

What I will pack with me:

TRAVEL ITINERARY
Things to Buy, Eat and Visit

DAY 1	
DAY 2	
DAY 3	
DAY 4	
DAY 5	

DREAM HOLIDAY

I am going to:

Why I chose this location:

How will I get there (conveyance):

Activities I will do with Him:

What I will pack with me:

TRAVEL ITINERARY
Things to Buy, Eat and Visit

DAY 1	
DAY 2	
DAY 3	
DAY 4	
DAY 5	

____________________________ *(your name)* knows it by heart she'll be going to these vacation with her twin flame in the near future and she keeps journaling about more dream destination to visit and visualize her romantic vacations every now and then.

INNER CHILD HEALING

With all the creative processes of the Law of Attraction _______________________
(your name) has been doing she realizes that she needs to do inner child healing and shadow work to clear her energy to manifest speedy harmonious union with her twin flame.

She realizes that she needs to release her repressed limiting beliefs and any memories of traumatic incidents which are keeping her in low vibration and creating blockages in her twin flame relationship.

One day she was reading that we need inner child healing if we've experienced the following below:

- Parents made you feel shameful about yourself or your actions.
- Have mother wound or father wound.
- Faulty attachment styles – Secure/ Avoidant/ Anxious
- Shame about the belief that you are broken from inside and need healing

- Emotionally unavailable parents
- Emotional or Physical abuse in childhood
- Lack of worthiness

If we experienced any of the above, remember that this had nothing to do with us. Release all these limiting beliefs and observe if we have any of them.
If we feel a deep connection with someone emotionally unavailable because it feels familiar with our childhood abandonment issue; or who's not choosing us, it's because we are not choosing ourselves.

She introspects about this and releases any maladaptive behaviour, choice or beliefs.
She creates a journal for inner child healing with therapeutic worksheets based on cognitive behavioural therapy.

**_______________'s Inner Child Healing
JOURNAL**

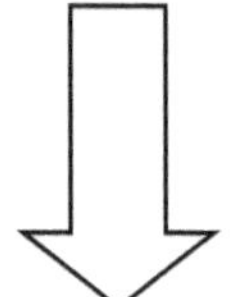

LIST OUT ALL YOUR CHILDHOOD TRAUMAS

Make a list of all childhood traumas and bad days that you remember and that have a significant impact on you to this date. E.g.- the death of a loved one, any upsetting incident from the past, physical or emotional abuse, separation, parent's divorce, karmic relationships, etc...

PREDOMINANT REPRESSED FEELINGS

Feelings are the emotions you experience in your body and heart. There are many different feelings that you may have, and your feelings may change from moment to moment. Sometimes you might even feel two or more feelings at the same time. There are no good or bad feelings, but there are positive and negative ways of expressing feelings. How would you describe these feelings? Are there colors associated with them? Can you think of a childhood traumatic experiences associated with regular and predominant feeling you experience on a daily basis?

____

____

____

____

____

____

____

____

____

____

____

____

____

OBSERVING FEELINGS IN YOUR BODY

One way to understand your emotions is by paying attention to your body. When something stressful happens, do you get a pit in your stomach? Or do your muscles get tight? Your body might give you signs to understand your emotions. You don't have to do all the feelings you listed; you can choose which feelings you want to include. For each feeling you choose, close your eyes or look down and imagine having that feeling right now. Where do you experience that feeling in your body? Please colour in the places on your body where you experience each feeling and draw and write what it feels like.

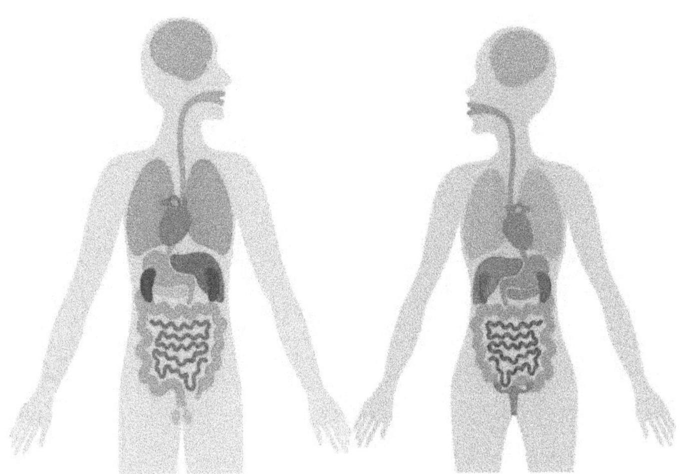

COPING WITH DIFFICULT FEELINGS

When you experience a difficult feeling very strongly, it is helpful to remember that emotions are temporary, and you will not feel this way forever. Feelings are like waves that come and go with highs and lows. But if you are feeling stuck in a low or feel like the waves keep crashing on your head, you can do things to lessen the intensity of the feeling. For example, if your anger is at an 8 (strong), you can do things to bring it down to a 1 or 2. What are some of these things you can do? Make a list of coping skills you can use to manage any of your difficult feelings.

____

____

____

____

____

____

____

____

____

____

____

WRITE YOUR HEART OUT TO A KARMIC PERSON WHO HURT YOU

Remember a person who hurt you and your emotion in childhood. Write their name and how they hurt you, what all you felt and complaints you wish to tell them for their wrong actions with you. Write out whatever comes to your mind. Picture the day they let you down or hurt you.

____

____

____

____

____

____

____

____

____

____

____

____

____

____

____

____

____

FORGIVE AND RELEASE WHOEVER HURT YOU

Make a list of people who hurt you and your emotion since childhood. Write their names and that you forgive and release them from your mind and that you no longer are the prisoner of your past. You take back your control from them and let go of them from your mind and soul. *Remember- forgiveness and letting go of trauma and perpetrator is a regular process, to completely release and cut the energetic cord with them. So, make it a habit to forgive.

____

____

____

____

____

____

____

____

____

____

____

____

____

____

CHALLENGE NEGATIVE THOUGHTS

When dealing specifically with anxious thoughts, worries or predictions it can be beneficial to ask yourself the following questions to help you gain a different, and potentially more fruitful, insight. Write down the answers for each of your distinct worries or thoughts.

Questions to challenge your worries or anxious thoughts:

How important will this be in my life 3-5 years from now?

____

____

____

____

____

____

____

____

____

____

____

What would my best friend suggest I should do about it?

____

____

____

____

____

____

____

____

____

____

What would I counsel my best friend to do if this was there an issue?

____

____

____

____

____

____

____

____

____

____

____

My way of assuming and seeing things is this only
one possibility?

____

____

____

____

____

____

____

____

____

____

____

Am I jumping five steps ahead when the first step
hasn't even happened yet?

____

____

____

____

____

____

____

____

____

____

Am I overestimating the chances of adversity?

____

____

____

____

____

____

____

____

____

____

____

Now think of some of your own questions to
challenge your worried apprehensive thoughts and
write them down. Feel free to write as many as you
like!

SELF ACCEPTANCE WORKSHEET

1. What is the issue or circumstance that you find tricky or difficult? What occurred before the childhood traumatic circumstance that emerged? How could it happen? How could it unfurl? Who was there? What feelings did you experience during this circumstance?

____

____

____

____

____

____

____

____

____

____

2. What role did your conduct play in this traumatic circumstance? What about other's conduct?
a) Describe your actions and behaviours during this experience and consider how your reaction affected what happened. Keep in mind, you can't control how others will act.

b) How did others' conduct impact the circumstance?
How did their actions add to what exactly occurred?

c) What were you able to control during this traumatic circumstance? What were you not able to control?

____

____

____

____

____

____

____

____

____

____

3. Consider and portray your responses to the childhood traumatic circumstance.   How could you respond, act, or carry on to what in particular happened? What impacts did your responses have on you inwardly? Recollect
that a reaction is thought of, purposeful conduct. A response, interestingly, is the point at which you permit feelings to control your conduct.

____

____

____

____

4. What was the effect of your response on others around you? Depict how they reacted when you responded the manner in which you did.

5. In what manner may you respond next time with the goal that you can limit your receptive reaction? How is it possible that you would react, rather than responding, to diminish your own emotional well-being?

____

____

____

____

____

____

____

____

____

____

____

____

GROWING STRONGER FROM THE DARK NIGHT OF THE SOUL

 Childhood trauma often leads to triggers of Clinical Depression, Anxiety and other mental conditions. The emotional turbulence regularly makes it hard for us to preclude where accurately the nervous breakdown began.   This Worksheet turns out best for individuals who have encountered different horrible mishaps throughout everyday life and Childhood. It permits you to investigate the strengths that you have used to adapt to the childhood Trauma and the new ones you've created thus. This worksheet is straightforward and incorporates queries to trigger strength-based reflection.

 5 Innate Strengths I had previously ?

____

____

____

____

____

____

____

____

____

____

Which strengths did I use to get past my Childhood Traumatic experiences?

New inner strengths I've developed over the past years?

____

____

____

____

____

____

____

____

____

____

____

Making us fully aware of a more adjusted, positive viewpoint on difficulty and childhood trauma in this manner regularly causes us to understand that we definitely know some fruitful systems for handling future challenges.

PROLONGED EXPOSURE THERAPY

According to the Cognitive Behavioural Therapy theory, as the avoidance of the memory is prevented, one has a chance to learn that it can no longer hurt, and desensitization occurs with the childhood traumatic experience. Many people want to evade whatever reminds them to remember the trauma they encountered, however doing so fortifies their dread. By confronting what has been kept away from, an individual can diminish the side effects of PTSD by effectively discovering that the trauma-related recollections and stimuli are not risky and don't need to be evaded.   This therapy involves having you to write and tell the story of the trauma memory in detail, along with thoughts and emotions, from beginning to end. And then write about it again, and again every alternative day (2-3 times a week) with more details as you recall.

____

____

____

____

____

____

LETTER TO THE PERPETRATOR WHO BROKE YOUR HEART

To: _______________________________

These are some of the things that I have been wanting to say to you. I used to think

____
____
____
____

and that you

____
____
_______________________________.

Then things changed. After you began hurting me, I thought that

____
____
____
____
____
____
____
____

and I wondered if

____
____
____
______________________________.

When I think of you hurting me, I

____
____
____
____

and I feel

____
____
____
______________________________.

You are

____
____
____
___________________________ and
____
__________.

Sometimes when I think of you I

____
____
____
____
______________________________.

I want to tell you that

____

____

____

____

____.

If I ever, or when I see you again, I will

____

____

____

____

____

and

____

____

____.

P.S.

____

____

____.

She released all her past resentments, trauma and negative beliefs related to her traumatic incidents through journaling. Doing all these self-healing therapeutic worksheets every week she felt light-hearted.

CLEARING ENERGY BLOCKS IN ULTIMATE LOVE UNION

After releasing all her past resentments, trauma and negative beliefs related to her traumatic incidents through journaling, _________________ *(your name)* works on her Good Qualities, Inner Self, Desires and Law of Attraction through journaling and makes notes about everything to clear blocked energy coming between her Twin Flame Reunion.

1) Trust in your Strength and Good Qualities:

Be Grateful for the positive aspects of yourself. The good traits you have makes you a nice and unique person. Sit down and focus on what you are grateful about your life and your core strengths.

Trust in yourself and your good qualities. If you do so, other people will also notice your attractive aspect and strengths, hence they will be allured towards you. Also, make a habit to feel whole and complete right now. Feel the emotions of being whole and complete and having whatever you desire already.

Sit down in a quiet place and write down the good qualities which make you the wonderful person that you are.

E.g.- I am a compassionate and helpful person and I'm there if someone needs support.

____

____

2) Welcoming The Happiness You Deserve:

Write down the type of people or partners you attracted in your past, and the red flags you saw. Make a list of those and affirm to yourself you are done with you being treated wrong or experiencing conflicts. *(These are not your conditioned type of thinking anymore)*
Then make a list of qualities you wish to experience in your ultimate lover.

Undesired Qualities experienced in ex-partners which will not be tolerated by you now:
E.g.- Being ignorant of my emotional needs and my presence in life. Take me for granted.

____

____

____

____

____

____

____

____

____

____

____

____

____

____

____

____

List of desirable qualities in your ultimate lover:
<u>E.g.- Communicating regularly and choosing me above everything else. Making me and our relationship his priority.</u>

3) 90% of your life is run by the subconscious mind.

Before and after sleeping feel all the emotions you want to experience, especially when in a committed relationship.

When we go to sleep we are going from the beta (brainwave) state to the alpha state then to the theta state and then to the delta state. Theta and Delta state is a very powerful brainwave state to reprogram your subconscious mind and induce a positive belief system and thoughts in your mind. Theta brainwave state is the best time to reprogram your subconscious and the Delta brainwave state is best for reprogramming with lucid dreaming.

After we were born till about the age of 10-12 we are mostly in the theta state, that's why we absorb beliefs and information very quickly. The subconscious mind understands the language of feelings and emotions. So, feel your desires already manifested by the universe, as if you already have them. Visualise having all that you desire daily when you're feeling relaxed with all the feelings and emotions.

Make a list of all that you want in life and wish to experience in and with your ultimate lover as if you already have it:

E.g.- <u>I am so happy and grateful now that my twin flame/ultimate lover expresses his love for me and we are in a committed relationship.</u>

You attract what you are, not what you want.
Don't try to enter or be part of their (twin flame)
life's movie, attract them in your life's movie. Be the
star of your movie. You'll become more magnetic to
attracting love and your ultimate lover.
Focus on your passions and yourself from that
energy state you'll attract the partner you seek.

Feel this before sleeping and after waking up in bed:
- ♥ *How will it feel to look in their eyes?*
- ♥ *How will their touch feel?*
- ♥ *How will it feel to go out with them?*
- ♥ *How will it feel to confide trust in them?*

This will generate the feeling of having them already
from within. Your ultimate lover and other people
will feel this magnetic attraction.

4) Let it go, and Let God. (Surrender Stage)

The moment you trust and surrender to the desired outcome, that's when you attract it. As you are not vibrating the feeling of lack.

When you start to live knowing you're whole and complete and with the feeling of your ultimate lover is already your (what's meant for you will always be yours and will not pass you by), that's when you attract your ultimate lover/ twin flame back.

Make a list of desires or limiting habits that you need to let go of and surrender to the universe:
E.g.- <u>I let go of anxiety and the constant need to check on whether I'm in union with my twin flame or not.</u>

5)   Are you overly attached to your desired outcome?

Vibrating the feeling of lack, being in agony and not feeling whole and complete are the signs of being overly attached to waiting for your manifestation of desire. Others will catch that vibe too, hence repelling your ultimate lover from committing to you.

People pick up vibes and if you are not feeling whole and complete it will repel your partner.

Write a letter of gratitude to the universe *as if* already having and living your desires with your ultimate lover:

Dear Universe,
I am so happy and grateful now that I am in a committed relationship with my twin flame.

7) Focus on the absence of your ultimate lover?

Letting go of the attention we have on the relationship we don't have right now will make you more out of alignment with the desire you're manifesting. So, invest in yourself. Enhance your career, practice self-care and self-love, do shadow work and inner child healing, meditation, grooming, etc...

Make a list of what you would like to achieve and do for yourself, which will make you whole, complete and empowered. Making you ready and magnetic for your twin flame.

E.g.- *I will exercise more to get healthy.*
I will take out time for the evening skincare routine. I'll work harder to get my dream career.

____

____

____

____

____

____

____

____

____

____

____

____

____

____

____

____

8) Limiting beliefs creating obstacles to your union?

Example – "I only meet an emotionally unavailable partner."

Let go of attachments to these negative limiting beliefs.

Make a list of limiting beliefs you think you have and have learned due to your past experiences. e.i. – *Lack of worthiness, etc…*

____

____

____

____

____

____

____

____

____

____

____

____

____

____

____

____

____

____

____

____

____

With self-realization, letting go of limiting beliefs and energy cleansing ________________
(your name) felt more and more liberated by her past energy and heaviness in her heart.
She felt very light-hearted.
She felt more whole and complete as a person.
She no longer felt a need for someone to complete her and make her happy.
She knows that she is connected energetically with her twin flame. She can feel his love from the bottom of her heart and knows she'll be in physical union with him.
Whenever her twin flame came to her mind she gave him love and light energetically. She no longer waited for his reply, union and him. She started trusting her divine timing and the universe's divine plan. She has trust that she'll be in union with her twin flame in the near future.

HEALING MY TWIN FLAME CONNECTION

___________ *(your name)* knew that difficulty or no communication relationship with her Twin Flame, heartbreak, or any resentment or blame towards her Twin Flame for anything due to their separation, can be changed through gratitude. Gratitude will magically improve any difficult relationship.

She believed that when we go through a difficult relationship or a challenging situation in a twin flame relationship, in almost all cases, we're not in the least bit grateful for our twin flame or any specific person. Instead, we're busy criticizing the other person for the issues we have with them, and that also means we don't have gratitude for their presence in our life.

Criticism is never going to create a better relationship, and it's never going to make your life better.

She knew that the more she blame her twin flame, the worse the connection gets, and the worse her life gets.

Whether it's a current relationship or a past relationship, if we repress and carry-on resentful feelings toward another person, practising gratitude will clear out those feelings. Why wouldn't you want to remove your resentful feelings about another person or your Twin Flame?

Bad feelings or resentments about another person burn your life, but gratitude will eradicate them!

One day ____________ *(your name)* find a tranquil place and make a written list of **ten** things she is thankful for about her Twin Flame. Remembering back through the history of their connection, and writing the great things about her twin flame or the great things she received in their relationship. The easiest way to do this is to remember the way things were before the relationship deteriorated or you both got separated.

If the connection had too many ups and downs or misunderstandings, then think hard about any good qualities in your twin flame because they are there.
This transformational practise is not about who is right or wrong.
No matter what you feel your twin flame has done to you, no matter what your twin flame said or didn't do, you can divinely heal the connection, and you don't need the other person in order to heal it.

There is good in every relationship, even the difficult ones, and to bring soul lessons and richness to all your relationships and your life, you have to find the good. As you dig and observe the soul lessons being taught by the universe in your difficult situations from the past or present, write it down, address the Twin Flame by their name, and express your sentence in gratitude:

_____*Name*_____, *I'm grateful for* ___*what?*___.

By the time she completed her gratitude
list of ten things, she felt much lighter
about her twin flame and the connection.
She knew the ultimate point she wants to
reach is that she doesn't have any
resentful feelings toward her twin flame
anymore because it was her life that is
harmed by those feelings.
She started seeing her connection starting
to transform miraculously before her own
eyes.
It only takes one person
to divinely transform a connection
through gratitude, but it is the person
who uses gratitude who receives the
benefits in their whole life.

_____Name_____, I'm grateful for ___what?___.

MANIFESTING ULTIMATE LOVER'S TEXT MESSAGE AND UNION

With the power of her strong belief and positive thinking, _______________[Your Name] decided to try a text manifestation technique to reconnect with her Twin Flame. She knew that the energy of her intentions could manifest the communication she desired.

Step 1: Creating the Contact

First, she added her own number to her phonebook with her Twin Flame's name or simply as '*My Love*' or '*Perfect Partner*'. This small step made her feel connected to him already.

Step 2: Crafting the Message

Next, she chose a simple and believable text message she'd like to receive from her Twin Flame. She typed the message, sent it to herself, and saw her Twin Flame's name pop up on her mobile screen. The sight of his name filled her with joy and anticipation.

Step 3: Visualizing and Feeling the Emotion

She allowed herself to have a happy emotional reaction to this text message as if her Twin Flame had sent it. She took a screenshot of the notification and text, and looked at it a few times per day, feeling the excitement and love each time.

By engaging in this practice, _______________[Your Name] anchored the positive energy and expectation into her daily routine without becoming desperate or overthinking. She maintained a happy and peaceful vibration, trusting that the text would come when she least expected it.

The Message Arrives

One day, while having lunch with her old friends, [Your Name] received a text message from her Twin Flame. Her heart skipped a beat as she read his words asking about her well-being. They began texting each other often, reigniting the connection that had been dormant for so long.

As they communicated more frequently, they decided to put effort into their relationship and make it work. They started meeting often, and her Twin Flame expressed how much he missed her and loved her. He confessed that he couldn't imagine his life without her anymore. He had come out of his shell and felt like a better person than before.

A New Chapter of Love

Their bond grew stronger with each passing day. They both realized how much they had grown individually and how their union was destined to help them grow even further. They planned a vacation together to celebrate their renewed relationship, a trip that marked the beginning of their new journey together.

Growing Together

With each passing moment, their relationship evolved, and their love for each other deepened. They supported each other's strengths and compensated for each other's weaknesses, becoming true partners in every sense.

Happily Ever After

And one fine, auspicious day, they walked down the aisle and entered into marital bliss. Surrounded by loved ones, they exchanged vows, promising to love, honour, and cherish each other for all time. Their journey from separation to union was a testament to the power of belief, self-love, and the unwavering connection of Twin Flames.

Their story was a beautiful reminder that love, when nurtured with care and patience, could overcome any obstacle. As they embarked on their new life together,
__________________[Your Name] and her Twin Flame knew that their love was truly destined, guided by the universe and strengthened by their unwavering faith in each other.

ABOUT THE AUTHOR

Jasmine Rana is a Spiritual Psychologist, Life Coach, Couple Therapist, and Lightworker who has dedicated her life to guiding individuals and couples on their journey towards inner healing, spiritual awakening, and harmonious union.

Jasmine specialises in Inner Child Healing, illuminating the path to healing deep-seated trauma and rediscovering the authentic self. Her expertise extends to assisting souls in their Spiritual Awakening, empowering them to embrace their true essence and purpose with clarity and conviction.
Her teachings are infused with the wisdom of the Law of Attraction, guiding individuals to manifest their desires and create a life of abundance and joy. Her approach to healing is holistic, encouraging individuals to embark on a self-healing journey that nurtures the soul and fosters holistic healing.

Through her insightful self-help books, Jasmine extends her wisdom and guidance to every household, making spiritual growth and transformation accessible to all. Her words resonate with empathy and empowerment, inspiring readers to embark on a journey of self- discovery, union with the ultimate lover, healing, and spiritual evolution.

If you're seeking clarity on your twin flame journey, love life, or any other personal matter, Jasmine offers personalized Tarot Card Analysis Reports. These insightful reports provide guidance and spiritual messages that can help you navigate your path with more confidence and clarity. Whether you're dealing with relationship challenges, personal growth issues, or seeking answers about your soul's purpose, Jasmine's Tarot reports offer valuable insights to support you on your journey.

To book your Tarot Card Analysis Report, visit [https://buymeacoffee.com/jasminerana/extras **].**

www.ingramcontent.com/pod-product-compliance
Lightning Source LLC
Chambersburg PA
CBHW040805120726
48005CB00012B/1304